Disa

The Inclusive Church Resource

DARTON · LONGMAN + TODD

First published in Great Britain in 2014 by
Darton, Longman and Todd Ltd
1 Spencer Court
140 – 142 Wandsworth High Street
London SW18 4JJ

ISBN 978-0-232-53065-0

A catalogue record for this book is available from the British Library

Phototypeset by Judy Linard
Printed and bound in Great Britain by
Page Bros, Norwich, Norfolk

Contents

Acknowledgements

Inclusive Church is grateful to all who have made this book possible.

In particular we would like to acknowledge the enthusiasm and support for this book from David Moloney at Darton, Longman and Todd.

This book arose from two Disability Conferences that St Martin-in-the-Fields and Inclusive Church ran together. The insights from these conferences were the springboard for this book.

We are grateful to the Churches Equality Practitioner Group for ideas and suggestions for this book series.

We would especially like to thank those who have generously given of their time and contributed stories, reflections and resources.

It is our hope that all that is shared here will encourage others to go further in the work of creating a more inclusive and welcoming church.

John M. Hull is grateful to the Westhill Endowment Trust and the Grimmitt Trust, both in Birmingham, whose generous grants made possible the research and writing of this text.

About Inclusive Church

Inclusive Church was formed in 2003. From the start, churches and individuals have signed up to the statement of belief as a way of indicating their desire to see a more accepting and open church.

The Inclusive Church 'Statement of Belief'

We believe in inclusive church – church which does not discriminate, on any level, on grounds of economic power, gender, mental health, physical ability, race or sexuality. We believe in church which welcomes and serves all people in the name of Jesus Christ; which is scripturally faithful; which seeks to proclaim the Gospel afresh for each generation; and which, in the power of the Holy Spirit, allows all people to grasp how wide and long and high and deep is the love of Jesus Christ.

www.inclusive-church.org.uk

Introduction

CLARE HERBERT

The Revd Clare Herbert is Tutor in Contextual Theology and Mission for the South East Institute of Theological Education. At the time of writing, she was a trustee of Inclusive Church and Inclusive Lecturer at St Martin-in-the-Fields.

> I am good at working alongside disabled people and have helped form two conference days with Inclusive Church at St Martin-in-the-Fields.
>
> I am lousy at working alongside disabled people and have helped form two conferences days with Inclusive Church at St Martin-in-the-Fields.

How is it possible that both these statements are true? To write the Introduction to this book in my role as trustee of Inclusive Church and priest on the staff of St Martin's gives me the chance to explore this contradiction. Living the contradiction has enabled me to understand the demands of inclusion in ways unknown to me when I was simply 'fighting my own corner' as a woman priest and as a member of the LGBTI community within the Church of England.

The first story is a success story.

Four years ago I had the immense good fortune of being appointed Lecturer in Inclusive Theology at St Martin-in-the-Fields. My task is to draw into the light groups of people who receive a warm welcome at St Martin's but who consequently remain in the shadows, unlikely to find a voice in organisational leadership, policy-making or the performance of liturgy. My employer was keen that I begin my new work by inviting a disability adviser to talk to our clergy team. Very little action arose from that pleasant evening event. We were given a list of things to think about which we had probably thought about already, albeit vaguely. I now realise that nothing much happened because none of us at that time had lived experience of disability. In a large, complex, fast-moving organisation that which is not considered urgent moves to the bottom of the list of priorities of the leadership team.

Confident, gifted congregation members with lived experience of disability were less prepared to remain voiceless. Over the past three years they have created a Disability Awareness Task Group (DATG) to tackle practical issues like access, and to host social and liturgical events within St Martin's. We have shared a splendid meal, sat at a candlelit liturgy, made a presentation to the church and assisted at a service for St Luke's Day. Our greatest sense of wonder and achievement, however, is gained from working together with Inclusive Church at two autumn day conferences called 'Opening the Roof' and 'Places of Belonging', which we hosted at St Martin's in 2012 and 2013. They are described at other places in this book.

Yet after two years' work we came to a halt, exhausted. What happened? This half of the story is less about success, more about failure. Yet strangely I sense that very failure will be where the new work of inclusion begins. The difficult work of inclusion is not solely about entrances and exits and spaces for wheelchair users to feel comfortable, vitally important as that work is. The difficult work is inner work. My experience suggests it is possibly that inner work which prevents the outer more practical work happening more quickly on behalf of disabled people in society and church.

The inner work is about slowing down. Do I have the time and the patience truly to understand this person with me who is very different from me? Before I began this work I believed that we are all basically the same, that I had been disabled by difficult experiences in some aspects of my being. I now think that is a false perception. Straight people are not gay, men are not women, and I do not have epilepsy or bipolar disease or arthritis. It simply does not help in trying to understand the other to own their lens, their way of seeing. With the help of a gifted work consultant I began to take time to understand my disabled colleagues in their particular personhood. To do that is not to expect the work to move so fast. Why are we in such a hurry anyway?

The inner work is about coping with anger. When I began this work I was outraged that my disabled colleagues vented such wrath around St Martin-in-the-Fields. Now I understand ... a little. When I add up what has happened to them most weeks in terms of benefit cuts, rudeness, means assessment, disablement from positions of empowerment, and frustrations in travel and communications, I wonder how they have made it to church at all. Then, if the door is locked, or face unfriendly, or lift not working again, the effects of the frustrations endured in the past week may be cumulative.

The inner work is about owning the self-centredness which may rest at the heart of our work on inclusion and nudging it aside. Because my disabled colleagues in the DATG and conference planning groups are very different from me they force me to consider what I am like when my hopes, pace, identity and self-assertion are not inevitably and quickly welcomed. In facing the violent feelings I sometimes encounter within myself when my particular wishes are thwarted, not suiting another's needs, I confront the sheer hard work which is inclusion. That hard work lies in coping with the inner fears which may threaten to overwhelm us. Bells may ring within us which make us wish to push away disabled people, or play down their disability, so painfully do they clamour. Meeting another's need is not immediately or glamorously or self-gratifyingly easy.

And isn't that the same with all areas of inclusion? The areas of hard work which slow us down as society and church are around our inner fears of women, or gay sex, or child's play, or unaccustomed ways of life, or inner chaos, or outer disfigurement, or death.

Work has begun again on further conferences, groups, events. What I have learnt is that inclusion cannot be commanded or rushed. It takes time and patience, honesty and stubborn determination to recognise what inner bells are ringing, to remove beams from eyes, and above all to listen to the particular difference of the other. It requires the breaking down of barriers and the growth of understanding, not of what is usually deemed 'normal', because none of us appears to be that, but of what is needed here, in this place, at this time, with this person, for welcome and exchange to take place. It requires nothing less than the recognition of that old spoiler 'enmity', and the replacement of hostility with love.

PART 1

Experience

Stories from lived experience are central to this book. It would be easy to skip this section and read the theological reflection or look at the resources. The stories here are real and speak of what it is like to live with disability in different forms. We are grateful to these storytellers for their honesty. Our theological reflection and practical outworking should follow from these accounts of lived experience, so please take time to read these stories carefully.

Susan's story

Susan Marina Wolfe is an American social historian, living in London. She misses the mountains, her garden and a dog (and horse and cats). She believes every creature, every person, has an inalienable right to live to its own potential, to be the best contented self, the best lizard or mayfly or human being or cuttlefish it can be.

This is for a childhood friend who died as an adult, not directly from epilepsy, but from an absence of love from those who did not understand.

My biggest problem with epilepsy is other people. I don't lose consciousness. I don't need medical attention when having a seizure. My arms jerk and my head jerks and my voice gets louder and sometimes I bark like a seal. I look weird.

People seem to think I can control what is happening to me. They often shout in my face or make fun of me. I've been dragged out of a building and thrown on to the street by the security guard to whom I went for help in finding a quiet place to sit. I didn't fit the only type of seizure he knew about. My seizures make other people uncomfortable. The type of seizures I have are triggered by particular sounds. Before this happened to me four years ago, I didn't know there were over 40 different types of epileptic seizures and that only 5 per cent are triggered by flashing lights. Some are triggered by sounds and some by smells and some by nothing at all. They just happen.

Epilepsy is not a mental illness. It's a neurologic condition, often caused by scar tissue in the brain. Everyone has an electrical charge going through the brain all the time. We see this on EEGs as brain waves. An epileptic seizure occurs when that normal electrical charge is multiplied by thousands of times. Nothing in its pathway through the brain works properly. When the whole brain is involved, the person will lose consciousness and fall down. This generalised type of seizure is what most people associate with epilepsy. It's the second most common neurologic condition in the world (after stroke) and yet most people, including me four years ago, know little about it. It's not exactly pretty.

I have simple focal seizures of the frontal lobe. 'Simple' means I don't lose consciousness.

'Focal' means it's limited to that part of my brain. They don't feel simple while they're happening. I'm aware of everything from start to finish, to the rest I need after it's done. I know, from experience, the sounds I need to avoid – the frequencies and rhythms which will cause me problems. It is not what you would expect. It is not loudness – it is frequency. Sirens have no effect. A group of people speaking quietly in an enclosed space, however, can set up a low frequency hum which can trigger a seizure.

I can't be near a saxophone, but can stand beside a bagpipe all day. Dissonant jazz is not OK. Stravinsky is not OK. Brahms and Elgar are fine. Construction noise is dangerous to me. The WHOOSH of a cappuccino machine ... You should hear the remarks I make to myself about people who can't just order a quiet cup of coffee and be happy with it! They have no idea I can't remain in the coffee shop because they want a cappuccino.

Walking down the street would be hilarious if it weren't so annoying. I open the door of one shop – music too loud – go to the next shop – too loud – and the next. By the time I ask them to turn it down and explain the reasons why and remind them of the Equality Act which requires them to make reasonable adjustment for a disabled person, I realise I don't really want to try on the jacket I saw from the window. Shopping is just too hard – so my clothes must last a long, long time.

So what's all this got to do with 'belonging'? What's 'inclusion' got to do with it?

My seizures began four years ago. A few years before that, I'd joined a large organisation I came to love. It was central to my life. I was asked to help with an annual festival. Everyone knows I'm the worst cook on the planet, but I can put cheese on a cracker with the best of them. I loved the talk and laughter in the kitchen, the delight in filling tables with the dishes we'd prepared. My cheese and crackers were right there among the rest. At Christmas, it's the family busy in the kitchen while the guests are at the table. That festival night, that plate of crackers made me 'family'. And then I developed epileptic seizures. The following year, in the week before the festival, someone in quasi-leadership said to me, 'They've commissioned a new piece of music for the festival. You ... probably ... shouldn't ... come.'

My confidence crushed, I allowed someone who barely knew me to make a judgement about what was 'best for me'. I missed the festival and all the preparation. The following year no one asked me to help. Or the next. No one in the organisation asked me to do anything. The 'family' was busy in the kitchen, as it were, and I was relegated to the status of 'permanent guest'. My ability to put cheese on a cracker in a kitchen filled with laughter was not affected by the onset of epilepsy. But this is how we are marginalised – one cracker at a time. We know people 'mean well', but as Martin Luther King said, 'Shallow understanding from people of good will is more frustrating than absolute misunderstanding from people of ill will' (*Letter from Birmingham Jail*, April 1963).

There's a head football coach at the University of Minnesota, my old alma mater in the States. Jerry Kill has had generalised tonic-clonic seizures on the sidelines in the stadium, in front of his team, the media and 60,000 fans. His coaching assistants quietly know the protocol to assure his safety. The game continues and Jerry's back in his coaching chair the next morning. He considers the seizures a distraction from the job at hand. Jerry's not hiding. The university, a Big 10 American football campus, isn't hiding him either. He tried to take some time off as head coach early in the 2013 football season, but was back in the locker room at halftime two weeks later and then back in the coach's box.

His team's relationship isn't with his epilepsy, it's with him, and 2013 was their winningest season since 2003.

There are so many disabilities – all around us – everyone. We're hard of hearing and we're profoundly deaf. We're partially sighted and totally blind. Young, old, palsied, epileptic, allergic, chronically ill and dyslexic. We're learning disabled, sound-sensitive, use wheelchairs and sticks, suffer emotional illness. When it comes to disability, just as in everything else, we're all snowflakes. We're all different.

In 2012, my church, St Martin-in-the-Fields and Inclusive Church, organised the first annual conference for Disability Inclusion at St Martin's. I was proud to be there and delighted to participate. John M. Hull, who writes in this book, asked at the conference, 'Is there a God of blind people? In all that light, is there a God of the darkness?'

Long before I actually came into the church from another tradition, I always had a soft spot for Jesus the teacher, Jesus the human being who, much like me, got fed up and headed into the mountains or boarded a boat on his own. He experienced joy and anger, friendship and betrayal – everything human. And when he died, he carried his wounds with him as he returned to walk the roads again he knew so well.

I'm wounded too. I was wounded by a brain injury. Three weeks ago I learnt that my childhood friend, from whom I was inseparable for years until my family moved away, had also developed epilepsy. I spoke with someone who knew him, someone who had avoided him for decades, and I know that my friend died, not from his condition, but from the response of others.

Inclusion matters. Acceptance matters. Laughter in the kitchen matters. Talking together about inclusion and acting together about inclusion matters. I think about my childhood friend, the golden-haired boy in America who loved to swim in the summer sun, loved his dog, his family, his books and me. When he grew and developed a condition that makes people uncomfortable, where did he find an accepting community? Where was his laughter in the kitchen?

For the lack of inclusion, a friend was lost.

This is for Larry.

Fiona's story

Fiona MacMillan lives in the present moment and has learnt to become an instant expert. A native Londoner, she is distracted by detail but would rather name than label. Fiona has learnt to live with the certainty of uncertainty, been blessed with the wisdom of solitude and is currently exploring her voice as a writer.

'You can't sit there – you're in the way. Wheelchairs sit at the front.'

The words shook me from my reverie of remembrance. I was at a friend's funeral, in the city-centre church we had both attended for many years. It was a difficult occasion for everybody. The loss of a long-standing member of the community, the private griefs becoming public roles, a public event; the desire to get things right spilling over into a moment's irritated direction. 'You can't sit there. You're in the way. Wheelchairs sit at the front.'

Funerals are always hard, but this was one of my hardest yet. I had known this person, though not well, for most of my life. He had died after a short illness during which my experience of pain management and of pacing limited energy, of wheelchairs and of blue badges had brought us closer together. It was good to be at the funeral but it had been so hard to actually get there. Ten o'clock on a Monday morning and I was already exhausted and in pain and spilling over with emotion. It was hard not to be able to slip into a pew to sit next to my friends. You can't sit there. The thoughts of lives lived and parallel journeys, of younger, healthier selves, of the many tiny things that I could no longer do. You're in the way. But wait – did she really expect me to sit right at the front, between the family and the coffin? That really would be in the way, and such an uncomfortable place to be. Surprised, shocked, saddened, I moved and sat at the side. Apart from the rest of the gathered congregation, I observed the service from a distance, bereaved of more than a friend.

Until my mid-thirties I was a very healthy person. I had a demanding but rewarding and exciting job, and a pretty hectic and full life, juggling parenthood, friends and family with being a very active member of the church, singing and calling in a ceilidh band. I cycled everywhere and delighted in juggling projects and ideas. I was full of life. Then a virus left me with overwhelming fatigue, pain and difficulty thinking. I had to give up first full-time work, then study, then pretty much everything, except parenting and church. I loved church for the worship and the singing and the community and the friends. And I loved it too for the opportunities it gave me to keep my skills alive, the chances to join in, the sense of having something to give which was welcomed, and of a place where I belonged. But five years of ups and downs and struggles ended with another illness, more disabling and confusing than the first, and everything began to change.

Most people's understanding of illness is that it is tidy, predictable and stable. But then everything seems tidier from the outside. My illness is definitely not tidy, no matter how you look at it. All I know for certain is that I have antibodies to part of my brain. After more than a decade I now know that at least some of medical science is simply careful, educated guesswork. Perhaps in another ten years there might be useful treatment, but for now I simply have to see what works and learn to live with how things are. My illness affects the physical and the cognitive and the sensory, gives me pain and spasms and fatigue and problems with mobility. It changes all the time, which is why no one really understands or keeps up with it – not my family nor my friends nor my doctor nor indeed me – and that is hugely disabling in itself.

Yet I don't see myself as a person with a disability. (And who would want to define themselves by a negative?) I call myself a person with a neurological condition. I call myself a person in a wheelchair, or a wheelchair user. That's about it. After 15 years I am rather tired of collecting labels, unless they are particularly helpful ones. I still struggle with the language of disability so I'm not surprised that others do too. It's not that people don't want to be inclusive, it's often that they don't know how, or try and get it wrong and then are reluctant to try again.

Or perhaps the discomfort around illness and disability is because unlike many other social distinctions, this is something which will ultimately affect everyone. People don't go to bed one day as women and wake up as men, or go to bed Asian and wake up white; they don't often discover they are actually straight rather than gay. But people living healthy lives now are generally not going to die as healthy people. The fragile nature of health and of life is almost the last taboo, and we who are already broken are an unwelcome reminder of the journey to come, a memento mori.

It is hard to get a sense of quite how different life becomes when not healthy, not able to move freely, think without struggle, or listen without pain. It is hard to explain quite how much my life is worn down by the constant drip of peoples' attitudes, assumptions and misunderstandings. It is hard to understand another's experience without sitting for a mile in their chair. Every time I leave the house – and I cannot leave the house without help – I am aware of both my effect on others and of their reactions to me. I have learnt not to leave the house without having saved energy to deal with what others will do; invariably if I do go out without this energy it is an uncomfortable experience.

As part of training my personal assistants I usually send the new PA out with the old, the experienced PA pushing the trainee in my wheelchair so that she gets a small sense of what it feels like to be pushed, to have no control over where you are going, to see the world from a different place and to feel the effect of people's responses. Invariably they come back with a sense of amazement and an awareness that they had never understood how uncomfortable I am, in every sense of the word. I wish there was an equally simple way of sharing the move from being engaged in the life of a community, valued and belonging, to being dependent, difficult and dispossessed.

There is something about living on the

edge of society, of the church, yet visiting these worlds which makes me feel like an ambassador to a familiar but foreign country, where I have some knowledge but need regularly to observe the different cultures and habits, events and people in order to translate, to fit in. After each visit I need time to reflect and remember in order to understand these other lives and places. Nowadays I am more comfortable with broken people, with those whose lives or minds or bodies have been disrupted, distorted; who no longer see themselves as in charge or impregnable. Invulnerable people are foreign to me, exhausting to be around because my attention slides off their smooth surfaces and has nowhere to rest. But broken people can be jagged yet have a gentle core of compassion, we share an unspoken recognition of our shared otherness. The light shines through the broken places in the most amazing ways.

And I have learned to be amazed, even while I am learning to be myself. I have had to relearn, this time at a visceral level, that my illness is not my fault; it is neither a moral failing nor something I have done and is not within my control. In the last few years I have begun to seek healing rather than to chase after cure, to try to really live where I am and with what I have. Despite all the difficulty and pain, I am no longer trying to change what I have, but to live more deeply within it, to trust that I am as I have been created to be, somehow. It is a journey from the outside to the inside and back again, to knowing and accepting myself, to using and learning from my lived experience in a way which I hope will transform it.

And mirroring that journey of self-acceptance and understanding is my experience in the church, in moving from a sense of belonging to displacement, from the centre to the distant edge. Perhaps now I have moved back to the edge of belonging and am beginning to move inwards, bringing what I now understand of difference, difficulty, disability; willing to share what I have and am and know.

I would like the church to know so many things, but chiefly something of how hard it feels to be vulnerable in this society right now. Everything we depend on is being cut – support services, transport, housing. Definitions of what it is to be disabled, to be too sick to work, are being changed to save money and for ideological reasons. Aggressive measures to tackle disability benefit fraud of less than 1 per cent are resulting in enormous hardship and suffering, in growing isolation and despair. And the church itself has cut or is cutting much of the funding for its work with disabled people, making awareness and understanding so much harder, change so much slower.

I want the church to know that, even post-Paralympics, it is still a hard world out there for those of us who are vulnerable. Each day is for many a struggle of pain, of fatigue, of confusion, of loss, of judgement, of blame, of impatience, of rejection. Do not be as the world, labelling and judging. Welcome us as you welcome each other, honour us as though we were the greatest guest, not the least to be squeezed in and suffered. Listen to us – we are not the same, we have lived different lives, have stories which are worth hearing. Look on the edge for the signs of life, for what belongs at the heart.

My friend's funeral was a low point – indeed, one of a series of low points – and things are a little different now. It's not that painful things don't happen, because they still happen on a daily and weekly basis – we are, after all, a city-centre church, a reflection of society in all its weakness and strength. But painful things are less painful in a church which is trying to know better so that it can do better; which is listening, open, more aware. There is hope of change at the heart, and I am drawn in; signs of acceptance if not yet of understanding, while the work of inclusion promises something of and beyond belonging.

Rachel's story

The Revd Rachel Wilson is a wheelchair user with cerebral palsy. She was ordained in 2012 and currently serves as Assistant Curate at St Edmund's Church, Dartford. She also works as an employment adviser for Jobcentre Plus and prior to ordination worked in a variety of roles in the private and voluntary sectors. She has two children.

Nobody is more surprised than I am that my life has taken the direction it has and that I find myself a priest in the Church of England. My surprise is not only that I find myself ordained, but that in answering that call to ordination I have found contentment I never thought possible.

I grew up in a nominally Church of England family without any real sense of an active faith, or of what 'being a Christian' really meant, beyond having the sort of seasonal and occasional contact with the church which was common to a lot of families of our acquaintance. As I grew into adolescence, my relationship with matters of faith became increasingly ambivalent; I was both intrigued by adults of my acquaintance whom I knew to be Christian, who appeared to 'have something I didn't' and increasingly suspicious of contact with churches who seemed far too ready to tell me that God loved me and wanted to heal me, in a way that was highly simplistic and deeply patronising. On reflection, my sense of frustration was probably magnified by being educated in a residential special school for physically disabled children. This meant that we were literally a captive audience for any well-meaning pastor, or vicar from a local church who wanted to come and minister to us; certainly the fact that I hated being educated in a segregated environment, something which was deemed necessary because I couldn't walk, did not make me feel warmly disposed towards people who said that God loved me so much he wanted to heal me! I remember commenting to a friend at the time that 'if there really was God, he wasn't very good at his job was he?'

During this period I dabbled with the school Christian Union but just ended up left with more questions than answers. By the time I got to university I had abandoned any notion that the Christian faith was credible; the zenith of this transformation must have been when I poured a pint of beer over a recently converted Christian friend, who said that 'if I prayed hard enough, I would be able to walk'. This of course was just dangerously misguided enthusiasm on his part, but from that point on, I in my turn demonstrated enthusiasm, in Pauline fashion, for 'breathing out murderous threats' against Christians; the irony of this reference is not lost on me – I had no idea who St Paul was at the time!

Eventually I married and had two children. Ironically, it never occurred to me that I wouldn't have the children 'christened'; it's what everyone does! Accordingly, my first child was baptised in the church where we were married, and to my shame I never really gave faith a second thought until my youngest child was baptised. The vicar insisted I came to baptism classes and also suggested my son might like to come to the toddler group; both prospects filled me with complete horror. I remember walking up to the church door to go to the toddler group, thinking 'I can't do this; that church is going to be full of Christians ...' Before I could change my mind, we'd been spotted and ushered in. Everything about me said, 'Don't look at me, don't talk to me and definitely, under no circumstances, mention the words "God" or "Holy Spirit"'; quite a big ask in a church, I grant you, but years of being got at by Christians had made me very wary of exposing myself to the 'Jesus loves you' dialogue again. There is in this, I am sure, a lesson for those of us who might be overly keen to share the love of Christ the first time someone disabled enters a church; 'being loved to death' is a terrifying prospect – just give people room to breathe.

In the midst of all this, I was still determined my son would be baptised, so I kept attending church, as I was required to do, and anyway he enjoyed toddler group, something that irked me at the time; I might have to admit that this church at least contained a few 'normal', even kind, people. Then, on 12 May 2012, something quite unexpected happened: I had a point of conversion. During the service on this particular Sunday morning, there was a teenager being baptised. This intrigued me – she was old enough to know her own mind, why was she doing this? Yes, I know I wanted my son baptised but he was a baby and I regarded that as entirely different! I still intended, even at this point, to have my son baptised and never go back to church.

However ... the vicar was preaching on Ephesians 2, 'for it is by grace, through faith you have been saved ...'.

> But God, who is rich in mercy, out of the great love with which he loved us even when we were dead through our trespasses, made us alive together with Christ – by grace you have been saved – and raised us up with him and seated us with him in the heavenly places in Christ Jesus, so that in the ages to come he might show the immeasurable riches of his grace in kindness towards us in Christ Jesus. For by grace you have been saved through faith, and this is not your own doing; it is the gift of God – not the result of works, so that no one may boast. For we are what he has made us, created in Christ Jesus for good works, which God prepared beforehand to be our way of life. (Eph. 2:4–10)

While this was being read, I felt myself getting hotter and hotter and I heard a voice somewhere behind my left shoulder saying, 'Rachel, I love you.' It was a feeling so tangible that I was certain other people must be able to see, but when I turned round to look, they were all oblivious. In that moment, in a way that I couldn't explain, I knew with certainty that God loved me. It is important to say here that just because I knew it, doesn't mean I understood it, at all.

In fact, in the weeks following this experience, while I was utterly convicted of the love of God, I was embarrassed and confused. Embarrassed because I'd had a point of conversion, something which previously I had been utterly dismissive of. More than that, my fledgling faith presented me with a problem: if you don't really believe in God, or at least not in a God who is interested, then you can attribute all the tough stuff of life, including disability, to fate, whatever that means, but once you *know* that God really does love you, completely, where does that leave you in thrashing out the tricky stuff?

Probably my greatest help in this, which was arrived at over months, was the fact that God was quite happy with me the way that I was, disability and all. However much it pains me to admit it, in the immediate afterglow of a new faith, there was something horribly seductive about the notion of being healed, about being able to walk, and it scared me. I still believe that God would be capable of putting me on my feet if he needed me to walk, but what he understood was that that was not the sort of 'healing' I needed; on the contrary, my healing came in the gentle reassurance that

God didn't think there was anything 'wrong' with me by virtue of disability at all; he loves me as I am and has created me as I am.

I know that for some of my friends, especially Christians, the notion that God intends me (this side of heaven at least) to be as I am is controversial, but it is something I am convinced of, and when I came to that realisation it was utterly revelatory; if I am indeed 'what God has made me', then I no longer have to worry about 'failing' to be like others, but can succeed in being myself.

Never was that realisation more important than when I felt the call to ordained ministry. It is important to say at this point that I used to have a debilitating stammer and my cerebral palsy means that co-ordination, balance and decent posture are never things I've got the hang of. Hardly surprising then that when I first thought that I heard the call to ordination, a feeling which simply wouldn't go away, I said to God something like, 'Look, God, I don't want to tell you what to do but I have to point out to you that I can't walk and can't speak properly – you can't be calling me into public ministry.'

God's answer was very clear – 'I know all that and that's why I'm calling you.' I am called because I am disabled, not in spite of it, and the knowledge of that is probably one of the most liberating and moving things I have ever experienced. To have my palms anointed at my ordination to the priesthood was a profound experience; you see, I can rarely get my hands to really do what I want, but God has chosen them to be put to work in the service of others.

When you grow up with a disability, the world is very ready to tell you that you're incapable, destined always to be in receipt of help, and my ordination has literally licensed, indeed mandated, me to work in the service of God and of others; the paradox of that in the face of my disability is glorious.

I hope that what I represent as a disabled priest will teach the church, and indeed people in general, that inclusiveness is about much more than the physical environment. Disability is not something to be 'allowed for' or excused but something to be truly embraced. I say this not as part of some sort of secular equality agenda but because each person who crosses the threshold of the church, disabled or not, is made in the image of God and is to be regarded as precious for that reason. It is the role of the church, first and foremost, to welcome people by virtue of their unique humanity, whoever they are, not because you might believe that as a disabled person I especially need to be 'looked after'. However unwittingly, if we are not careful, such all-encompassing kindness can become oppressive. We must allow disabled people to grow within the church, to become the people God has intended them to be; that includes allowing them the room to question, to make mistakes, to be angry, to be dismissive, in common with their brothers and sisters. I believe that if disabled people were allowed to truly flourish in the service of the church, in whatever capacity, then the effect would be transformative. For me, one of the greatest tragedies of the Inclusive Church agenda is that it has become purely synonymous in the public mind with issues of sexuality, or little more than a secular equality agenda with 'church added'. This is a profound mistake. In all the areas in which it operates, the Inclusive Church agenda should be recognised as being about acknowledging the fullness of God at work in all people, whatever their circumstances. I have been truly liberated and have come to be blessed in the service of the church, but the church must continue to strive to work with that vision and not against it.

In that way I pray that all churches will

eventually become places that are inclusive, places where all people can grow, not because they've signed a mission statement but for no other reason than they recognise that they work in the service of Christ and it is Christ who calls us to welcome, nurture and walk with all people, unconditionally.

Ben's story

Ben Allison is 27 years of age, dyspraxic and high-functioning autistic. He is currently training at Cranmer Hall, Durham, to be a priest in the Church of England. Ben lives with his wife of seven years, Clare, and their children, Amos and Alethea.

My disability is stealthy, I have no chair, or stick, or missing limb to mark me out. Indeed for the first 18 years of my life the thing I now call 'disability' was invisible even to me. There was always a certain 'oddness' about me; words and phrases like 'scatter-brained', 'eccentric', 'nutty professor', 'distracted', and sometimes just plain 'lazy' have followed me throughout my life. But when the label 'dyspraxic,' and later 'autistic', were applied to me, I finally felt that here were words that my 'oddness' could truly inhabit. I felt like I had found words for what I could not see or understand in myself. So many times in my life I felt like I was living on another planet, and now I understand that the 'world' of dyspraxia and autism really is removed from most people's experience of life.

Dyspraxia affects the way that your brain and body talk to each other, the normal connections are distorted. I lack proprioception, the sense of where different parts of my body are in relation to each other, making me clumsy and uncoordinated. My other senses are affected, making it difficult for me to process large amounts of sensory information, particularly my sense of hearing. This means that in crowded or noisy environments I struggle to pick out a particular 'thread' of speech or noise. Dyspraxia also affects the way that memories are formed, particularly affecting my ability to hold on to auditory information through what is spoken to me. I have what is known as a 'non-linear' mind: rather than following cycles or step-by-step progression, my thoughts expand in multiple directions, often with multiple starting points. I make logical flips and leaps that non-linear thinkers find hard to follow or understand. The autistic spectrum is precisely that, a spectrum, and I am definitely at the milder end of that spectrum. But combined with the fact that my dyspraxia means that I lack the muscle memory for the fine motor movements required to convey my feelings through my facial expressions and tone of voice, I find it difficult to communicate with people face to face. My autistic tendencies mean that I can easily suffer from 'sensory overload' if exposed to too many sensory elements all at once. I am often brutally and inappropriately honest. I get impatient and frustrated when people ask me questions whose answers seem obvious, and when people do not understand the message that I am trying to convey, or I am unable to articulate it. I have strong coping strategies in place to keep the effects of my disabilities to a minimum: I practice facial expressions in front of the mirror; I practise my tone of voice using a dictaphone; I read books on body language; I use relaxation strategies to reduce my anxiety and frustration in social situations, and I try really hard not to be too honest or talk too much about the things that excite me.

All the things I have mentioned above I see through the eyes of those around me, through my own eyes and through the eyes of the world. But God looks on me with the eyes of a father, the same way as he looked at Jesus. Jesus too was honest, not neurotypically honest, 'You smell lovely today, is that a new perfume?', but properly, autistically honest, 'You smell of bacon, I like bacon, but only the crispy smoky kind, the soggy wobbly stuff is yuck, and you do not smell like that.' Jesus is so inappropriate, he spends all this time with the wrong sorts of people, and he does not respond to earthly authority. For example, in Luke 11:37–54, Jesus gets invited to the house of a Pharisee to dinner, and not only does he not bother to wash his hands, he insults the Pharisee who points this out, 'Well at least I am clean inside.' Then, when some lawyers present suggest that he might also be insulting them with what he is saying, he agrees! Jesus was also as obsessive as any autistic person I have met. Is there any moment or conversation in the Gospels that Jesus does not turn into something about his own personal obsession, the Kingdom of God? He talks about it at dinner, on the road, in a boat and up a mountain. Jesus, like all true autists, just does not know when to shut up. Jesus was also, I believe, history's greatest non-linear thinker – in his very nature an inverted incarnation of what God was supposed to look like, tearing open the old Testament and tearing off in hundreds of directions with it at once, jumping from seeds to kingdoms, from five to five thousand, from life to death and back again.

I grew up in a Christian family, my dad is a vicar, I have always felt a strong sense of faith in Jesus Christ, I have a Christian wife, I take my two young children to church every Sunday, I am training to be a vicar myself, but I still feel uncomfortable attending church as a dyspraxic, autistic Christian.

So how has the church got it wrong? How has it managed to miss out on preaching a Jesus whose gospel is so obviously inclusive to people like me? Why do I feel so excluded so often by my people, my church? Let me tell you what happens when I walk into the church, the church that I would call my own, the church where I would wish to be included, the church where I would like to belong.

I have counted the number of pillars, I have counted the number of pews and I have counted the number of people in them. I have seen the imperceptible flicker of the light on the twelfth pillar. I have noted from the stonework the various phases of construction the building has gone through. I know that the rest of you don't see it, but just because you cannot see it does not mean it isn't there.

I have heard the inaudible whine that the spotlight on the fifth pillar is making. I have heard the mutter of some crossed radio-frequency through the microphones. I have heard rustling papers, rustling robes and rustling people. I can hear the rhythmic tapping of my fingers against the back of my hand. I know that the rest of you do not hear these things, but just because you cannot hear it does not mean it isn't there.

Then there are the people: people whose

names I'm expected to remember; people with strange habits, strange sounds and strange smells; people I'm expected to touch as we say the Peace; people I'm expected to smile at and talk to after the service. There are things that I am expected not to do: not to answer truthfully; not to tell them how I am when they ask me; not to talk at length about the things that I am passionate about; to pretend I'm interested when I'm not. There are people who I think are my friends, but can never be sure, everyone is so very nice to each other all the time. Then there is the sympathy, the tilt of the head when I tell them about my disability, the offers for prayer (Prayers for what? That I stop being me?), and the confusing attempts to play down the issues I have, 'Oh well, everyone is a bit forgetful!' I know that they do not understand me, and that I do not always understand them, but just because you cannot understand it does not mean it isn't there.

Kat and Alex's story: a partner's perspective

Kat Cumber is a teacher of Religious Studies and History in a comprehensive school. Married to Alex, a Church of England priest with multiple physical and neurological differences, she has also been his main carer for a number of years. Kat survived six years of theological education and this, along with her (very) mixed-race heritage has led her to believe fundamentally in the inclusion of all people. She also has a soft spot for John Barrowman and all things sci-fi.

It's interesting watching 'inclusion' from the sidelines. It's interesting, but frustrating to watch how the non-disabled deal with disability. First of all it has to be said that unless someone is actually in a wheelchair or has a limb missing it is beyond many people to comprehend that there is a disability at all.

In our experience of a person with disability training for full-time ministry, you are confronted with the question of what sort of pension risk you are likely to be with all your complex needs. How much support are you going to need to do your job? You clash with your boss because you see the world in a more black and white way than he does and you just can't stand injustice. You try to get to places on time, but you can't find your way. One problem after another – all related to your disability, but your boss just doesn't get it. So they extend your probation.

Finally you find somewhere where people accept you as you are. They may think you're a little eccentric at times, but they welcome you with open arms and they celebrate your creativity and the things you're good at while supporting you where you need help. You thrive and blossom.

Unfortunately when it's time to move again you are not so lucky. Gradually the man with a stick who desperately needs help, which is not forthcoming, but struggles on while people ignore what is needed because it is too much hassle, becomes the man in a wheelchair. The things that he needed to have done to make his work possible several years ago still haven't happened and the message is loud and clear – that one is broken, we're not getting value for money. He can't work at the pace of one that is not broken, he can't visit people at home. Funeral directors don't want to give him funerals because he is too stark a reminder of the mortality of mourners.

Worst of all he doesn't dress the part – after all that's more important than valuing the gifts that God gave him, which make him so good at what he does, so approachable to people who don't normally fit. He doesn't quite keep the admin as the organised people like it. Oh, and he won't pipe down when he's not happy about injustice. That stubborn, autistic streak that makes him say and do things that aren't 'normative' won't allow him to pretend things aren't happening. Will keep prodding away until someone does something.

And this is where we find ourselves today. The only 'choice' is medical retirement, because, while the wheels scare them, this neurodiversity is more than the 'normal' people can cope with.

PART 2

Theology

Theology of Disability

JOHN M. HULL

Each book in this series contains a substantial theological reflection by an expert in the field. Here John M. Hull helps us reflect theologically about disability, providing us with a map whereby we may perhaps be better informed about the subject, and begin to explore a theology of disability for ourselves.

JOHN M. HULL is honorary Professor of Practical Theology in the Queen's Foundation for Ecumenical Theological Education and Emeritus Professor of Religious Education in the University of Birmingham. He is totally blind, having lost sight in 1980, and has written extensively about blindness.

CHAPTER 1

Why theology of disability?

Theology is sometimes described as faith in search of understanding. Disabled people in the churches often find themselves in a search for understanding in two senses. First, people with disabilities often need to find a way of understanding their own lives. If they are people of Christian faith, the need for understanding can become more demanding. If you have a completely secular outlook on life, there is a statistical probability that so many babies will be born with unusual genetic inheritances; so many people will be involved in road accidents; so many people will experience severe and lifelong impairments. If you are a person of faith statistical answers may not be enough. You may wonder why the loving God did not arrange things in a different way, why prayers were not answered, why Bible readings and hymns are sometimes perplexing rather than clarifying. If Christian people with disabilities have such thoughts, the same is true of people in church who are not disabled. Indeed, sometimes the questions asked by friends and loved ones are more urgent and poignant than those asked by disabled people themselves. Why did God not heal our disabled minister? If disabilities are evil, why does the power of prayer and the presence of God often not make much of a difference?

There is a second sense in which understanding is necessary. We speak of someone as being a sensitive and an understanding person. We pray the prayer of St Francis that we should seek to understand rather than to be understood. Human understanding is produced by empathy, by being able to see the world from the point of view of the other. Without understanding from others we become more solitary, but friendship implies the gift of understanding. This is a particular problem for disabled people in church life because of the apprehension and embarrassment with which they are sometimes regarded by their fellow Christians.

Theology searches for understanding in both these senses. Theological thinking helps us to look calmly and deeply at the faith the church has inherited, and a transformed faith can free us from our fears. As our interior pain becomes less, we become more receptive to the pain of others.

Creating a theological map

We will be able to find our way around theology if we have a map. If we can get a bird's eye view of the whole region, we may be able to focus upon the area we are interested in, that of disability theology.

To create such a map we could distinguish three types of theology: branches, genres and frontiers. There are certain subjects which all Christian theologies have in common, although different traditions may place emphasis upon one aspect rather than others. These would include beliefs about God, Jesus Christ, human destiny and futures such as the afterlife and the last judgement. Let us describe these as branches of theology. Within each of these branches there are other areas, a bit like small branches coming off the main ones. So beliefs about Jesus Christ would include the incarnation, crucifixion, resurrection, ascension and his coming again. Human destiny would include beliefs about sin, forgiveness, transformation and so on.

Genres of theology refers to the way that particular approaches to theology arise from the circumstances of certain people. For example liberation theology is a kind of theology which arose in a situation of terrible oppression and injustice; black theology seeks to interpret the history and experiences of black peoples in the light of Christian faith; and feminist theology presents a particular interpretation of Christian faith which expresses women's experience. These genres of theology spring from marginalised groups who seek equality but it is also true that European theology itself is a genre, and we may speak about the typical theology of white people, or even of white men.

This brings us to frontier theologies. Here we should refer to the ways in which Christian faith seeks to interpret some area of human life which lies outside Christian faith, or which seems at first sight to lie outside. Examples might be theologies of money, of film, of history and so on. Money would not normally be thought of as a theological concept. It has its place in economics, dealing with prices, values and exchanges. But Christian faith might reflect upon the fact that money has some God-like qualities. It is universal, transcends space and time, is a focus of power, and it attracts human love. In a similar way, the producers of films do not necessarily think of their work as being religious except when it involves an explicit biblical or religious theme, but a thoughtful Christian might ask about the values implicit in certain films, the assumptions a film makes about power, meaning and love, and beginning like this, one might develop a theology of film. So also disability in itself need not necessarily be considered religious. In medical schools there may be a specialisation in disability rehabilitation and disability may be studied from a political and an anthropological point of view. But a thoughtful Christian might want to ask about the meaning of disability and some of the ways in which the very presence of disabled people seems to raise questions about faith, hope and love. So on our map of theology we have theological frontiers, or perhaps we might call them applied theologies, and one of these is theology of disability.

At this point you may be asking whether there can be a theology of a table leg. Well, the idea of a theology which seeks to interpret something in the world becomes ridiculous if you apply it to a tiny detail. It would be silly to try to have a theology of a table leg. Even a theology of tables would still be peculiar, but one could certainly develop a theology of creation in which the preservation of the Amazonian forests would be part of human responsibility as given by God. This is why it is so important to have a map which is on a fairly large scale. Like any map, if you examine it in too great a detail, you begin to lose the very perspective which the map is supposed to give you.

The distinction between branches, genres and frontiers of theology is not the only way you could colour the theological map, but it is certainly one way and it leads us into an understanding of what a theology of disability might be.

Disability as a branch, a genre and a frontier of theology

Now we have our map. Let us see how we can put disability on to it in several places.

Theology of disability is necessarily involved with the various branches of theology. For example, we might ask why the creator God did not perfect the human genetic inheritance so as to make sure that there were no inherited impairments. We might ask whether human disabilities are a product of the fall of sinful humanity. We might wonder what the meaning of the healing miracles of Jesus Christ might be for disabled people, and whether in the next world all disabilities will disappear. So we see that questions about disability draw us into the doctrines of creation, the nature of the human being, the work and person of Jesus Christ, the future life and so on. It is probably true that there is no branch of Christian theology which is not challenged by the questions raised by impairment and disability, and we will discuss some examples in Chapter 3. In return, the Christian meanings of disability require the insights of all those various branches of theology. The relationship is mutual, and the same would be true if we tried to create a theology of politics or of ecology or of childhood. Our understanding of childhood would be changed and so would our understanding of Christian faith. This is because Christian faith offers to give meaning to every aspect of life and in return Christian faith is enriched by every human experience.

Theology of disability might also be thought of as a genre of theology. We saw that many of these have arisen as various groups of people have felt that the mainstream Christian tradition has marginalised or even oppressed them. Liberation theology seeks to overcome the oppression of rampant capitalism. Black theology seeks to challenge the claims of white supremacy, and to throw light upon the history of black enslavement. Feminist theologians have shown that the outlook of the Bible is very largely patriarchal. They have sought to interpret the Bible from a female point of view, and have gone on to show that the church and its theology have been male dominated.

Disabled people also form a marginalised or disadvantaged group. In the United Kingdom, the unemployment rate among disabled adults of working age is twice as high when compared with the employment of non-disabled working-age people. Disabled men have a pay gap of 11 per cent when compared with their non-disabled peers, and disabled women have a pay gap of 22 per cent compared with non-disabled working women. Around a third of all disabled adults aged 25 to retirement are living in low-income households. This is twice the rate of that for non-disabled adults. People on low pay or in poverty are more likely to become disabled, as are people with a lower level of educational attainment.[1] It is not surprising that there is a worldwide movement on the rights of disabled people, and many governments have recognised this.[2]

Because it seeks to overcome disadvantage, theology of disability may be thought of as a theological genre. Like black theology, it seeks liberty and equality. Not all disability theology, however, falls naturally into this place.

You may remember that there was an area on the theological map called frontier theology.

[1] These facts are taken from the report *Disability in the United Kingdom 2010*, published by the Papworth Trust, http://www.papworth.org.uk/downloads/disabilityfactsandfigures2010_100202152740.pdf.

[2] In the UK, the Disability Discrimination Act, passed in 1995, is now included within the Equality Act 2010.

Some theologies of disability may be located here. There is a sense in which we may look upon disability as a human reality which can be interpreted by Christian faith. In the same way we may look upon sexuality and sexual orientation as features of being human, and these also may be considered in the light of Christian faith.

We may thus think of disability theology as an hermeneutic activity rather than as necessarily seeking liberation. Hermes was the Greek god who had wings on his sandals and on his helmet. His job was to carry messages from the gods down to humans. He was the interpreter of the will of the gods. From his name we get the idea of hermeneutics, which is the art or the discipline of seeking to understand or interpret the sacred scriptures. From this biblical origin, the idea has spread more widely. In encyclopaedias of science one may find articles on hermeneutics since all scientific data require interpretation before they can be understood. In the same way, theology of disability seeks to interpret the human reality of being impaired. There are theologies of disability which help disabled people find a deeper understanding of their lives. We take disability which is not obviously a religious category and interpret it in the light of faith. So in disability theology, Christian faith looks out beyond itself towards the human reality of impairment.

Let us sum up. Disability theology interacts with the various branches of theological study. It asks about the implications of various doctrines for human infirmity and impairment. Disability theology may also be thought of as a genre. As a genre, it seeks to champion the needs of disabled people, and to expose the ways in which the Christian faith itself or the Bible may create negative attitudes towards disabled people. As a frontier activity, theologies of disability may seek to interpret the human experience of disability so as to break down the barriers between disabled and non-disabled people, to interpret the meaning of the experience of disability and to include disabled people more fully within Christian faith.

We have now spread out before us a map of the theological country and we have located the various places where theology of disability may be found. Let us now begin to consider the actual content of disability theology.

CHAPTER 2

Disability theology as a genre of theology: denunciation

Let us begin by thinking of disability theology as one of the genres of theology, a bit like black and feminist theology. What such theologies have in common is their demand for justice. This involves the removal of obstacles which prevent people from obtaining equality. These obstacles might be economic, legal or historical. Others might lie in the attitudes or misunderstandings which deprive people of dignity or opportunities.

This means that theologies of this kind will have negative features as well as positive ones. First one must denounce, then one can announce. In the case of disability theology, the most obvious way into this is to examine how disabilities are spoken of. In general, the terminology has become more tolerant and accepting. People who could not walk used to be called cripples; today it has become more usual to describe such folk as being physically disabled. People who today would be called severely intellectually disabled used to be described as being feeble-minded, retarded, morons, imbeciles or idiots. The language seems to be continually changing as new sensitivities emerge. People with disabilities used to be called 'the disabled'. In this expression the person is absorbed into the disability so that groups of people would be described as 'the deaf' or 'the blind'. It is now more usual to use expressions such as 'blind people' or even 'people with blindness', although I myself find this rather forced. I once heard a blind friend say, 'I am not blind; I am a person one of whose many characteristics is blindness.'

Sometimes people dislike the expression 'disabled' because of its apparent negativity. People with disabilities are described as being 'challenged'. Those with physical disabilities are 'physically challenged', and blind or partially sighted people are 'visually challenged'. As for myself, a person with no light sensation at all, I do not regard myself as visually challenged. I am just blind! 'Differently abled' is another way of avoiding 'disability'. Sometimes people who are not disabled are described as 'temporarily able bodied', in order to break down the hard-and-fast distinction between people by emphasising that most of us will ultimately become disabled. One must also remember that many, perhaps most, disabilities are not visible. People may suffer from migraine, or from depression or from epilepsy, all of which can be profoundly disabling conditions.

I suppose it is important to ask who uses the terminology and why. Is it used by people with impairments or does it come from the wider public, perhaps from the caring professions, who are seeking always to speak in more respectful terms? One must always remember an important slogan of the American disability rights movement: 'Nothing about us without us'.

Interesting distinctions can be made between the words 'impairment', 'disability' and 'handicap'. Impairment is often regarded as a neutral expression, simply indicating that some part or aspect of a person's mental or physical life is not functioning well. If the special problems created by impairment are not recognised by society such that the person with the impairment is placed at a disadvantage, then the impairment would become a disability, and if the limiting impact of the disability were not overcome, the result would be that the person would become handicapped. If for example my ability to walk is impaired I could find myself disabled in trying to get around. A wheelchair would solve many of those problems. So I might say that although impaired, many of the disadvantages of my impairment had been overcome, and I am no longer disabled. If I then attend a conference in a building with no ramps and no lifts then I would be denied access and would be handicapped in my ability to participate in the conference. What stops me participating is not my impairment but the built environment, which was created by people who could walk.

I think there are particular problems in describing blindness and deafness. This arises from the fact that the English language, and perhaps all languages, use 'blind' and 'deaf' metaphorically in negative ways. The negativity is so deeply engrained in the metaphors that they are used habitually and unconsciously. So blindness is used to mean insensitivity, stupidity, a failure to distinguish, and ignorance.[3]

Unfortunately, many of these problems are made more acute by the Bible. The negative metaphor of blindness is particularly vivid in the Fourth Gospel. The account in chapter 9 of the restoration of the sight of the man born

[3] A number of the chapters in my *The Tactile Heart: Blindness and faith*, London: SCM Press, 2013 discuss these problems.

blind is the most widely discussed example.[4] The restoration of sight is an extended metaphor for conversion to Jesus Christ. Towards the end of the chapter Jesus says, 'For judgment I have come into this world, so that the blind will see and those who see will become blind.'[5] In the case of the man born blind, the words of Jesus were literally true: the blind had received sight. But if we insist upon the literal meaning, then it will be difficult to explain why any blind Christian had not received sight, and indeed this is a thought which puzzles some people. In some of the large congregations in the United States where the lifestyle of the pastor shows the way in which God will bless the most faithful Christians, it might be difficult for the congregation to understand that their pastor had remained blind, although I expect there are exceptions. As for the idea of those who see becoming blind, this must refer to people who, having been confronted by the challenge of Jesus Christ, reject him. They have become, so to speak, blind to the truth.

In the following verse the Pharisees ask Jesus, 'What? Are we blind too?', which is obviously metaphorical since they were sighted

[4] John M. Hull, *In the Beginning there was Darkness,* London: SCM Press, 2001, pp. 49–52.

[5] John 9:39

people. The reply of Jesus is puzzling: 'If you were blind, you would not be guilty of sin.' If we take this literally it would be referring back to the start of the story where Jesus declared that the man's blindness was not because of sin. It seems more likely, however, that what Jesus means is that if you have not been a follower of Jesus because of your ignorance then it would not be your fault. Jesus continues, '... but now that you claim you can see, your guilt remains'. Blindness is equivalent to sin and guilt. In claiming to see (to have knowledge and insight) the Pharisees have only displayed their self-deception and their persistent refusal to believe Jesus.

It is difficult to deny that the metaphor of blindness is used throughout this chapter in a negative sense. Nevertheless, some people do deny it. Amos Yong, for example, suggests that western society is dominated by ideas of normality. He describes these attitudes as 'normate': '[N]on-disabled people have a built-in *normate* bias against people with disabilities. This is a generally unquestioned worldview that functions subconsciously or unconsciously.'[6] This, he believes, helps us to understand why many people, influenced by their normate presuppositions, read even what

6 Amos Yong, *The Bible, Disability and the Church: A new vision of the people of God*, Grand Rapids, MI: Eerdmans, 2011, p. 11.

the Bible says about disability in a disparaging way. Yong describes his own work as follows.

> What this book provides is an honest discussion of the many texts that have been read as stigmatizing disabilities so that we can become more aware of how our biases and discriminatory attitudes have been historically justified, and how these prejudices remain, to this day, based both implicitly and explicitly on such misconstruals of the Bible.[7]

In discussing John 9, Yong says that he will use an 'hermeneutics of blindness', explaining that he will read the story of the man born blind 'from a non-sighted perspective'.[8] He believes that the negative association of blindness with ignorance and disbelief is not in the text of John but is projected into the text by the normate presumptions of the readers. 'My claim, however, is that the metaphor of blindness works inexorably toward such conclusions only for those who either cannot or do not question a sighted perspective.'[9] In this

[7] Yong, *The Bible, Disability and the Church*, p. 8.

[8] Yong, *The Bible, Disability and the Church*, p. 49.

[9] Yong, *The Bible, Disability and the Church*, p. 55.

way Yong refuses to admit that the text itself contains this negativity. His exposition of the way the normate assumptions marginalise disabled people is undoubtedly true and is well done, but he fails to see that the Bible itself shares the assumptions of the normate world. Yong does not discuss some of the most obvious cases of this negativity. For example, in Matthew 23 Jesus describes the Jewish leaders as 'blind guides' (v. 16), 'blind fools' (v. 17) and 'you blind men' (v 19).[10] Are these not negative? Is not Jesus, according to the Gospel text, using the word 'blind' to mean ignorant, stubborn and foolish? It is not a normate projection which reads these expressions in a negative way but a biblicist prejudice which is unable to acknowledge the fact that in the Gospels blindness is consistently used in a negative sense.

Of course, one might reply that these are only metaphors. Yes, but they are metaphors taken from the sighted world and used to marginalise and stigmatise blind people. It takes a genuinely blind hermeneutics of the Bible to recognise this because without the lived experience of blindness one either does not

[10] John M. Hull, 'Difficult Texts: Matthew 23.16–26 – blindness as a term of abuse', *Theology* 117:1 (2014), pp. 34–6.

notice these negative metaphors or one finds some way of avoiding their obvious meaning.

Another disability theologian who fails to recognise the negativity of the metaphors about blindness is Hans Reinders. This is related to his failure to recognise the positive metaphor of sight and seeing. He says, 'The fact that the eyes of a blind person are shut out from light does not at all imply that this person cannot see.'[11] In this sentence, the reference to blind people who cannot see is clearly literal, but the reference to still being able to see is obviously metaphorical. In the English language 'to see', in addition to the literal reference to the use of the eyes, is used to refer to knowledge, understanding and recognition. Reinders continues, 'In fact, the language of "seeing" referring to mental states is not metaphorical at all: it refers to a different way of seeing. The images I see in my mind are properly seen, only not with my eyes.'[12]

I take the view, however, that we should distinguish more carefully between the metaphorical and the literal senses of these words. The expression 'different ways of seeing' can be used quite literally. If a sighted person

[11] Hans S. Reinders, *Receiving the Gift of Friendship: Profound disability, theological anthropology, and ethics,* Grand Rapids: Eerdmans, 2008, p. 331.

[12] Reinders, *Receiving the Gift of Friendship,* p. 332.

looks at a room while lying flat on the carpet, this might be a different way of seeing, that is, a different perspective or angle. But when reference is made to the 'inner eye' or to 'seeing with the heart', one is no longer speaking of literal sight but in metaphors. The connection between sight and understanding is so intimate that it probably takes the shock of total blindness to realise it clearly. When Reinders said that the images in his mind 'are properly seen' he is speaking not as a profoundly blind person but as a sighted person with closed eyes.

When as a sighted person you close your eyes, of course you continue to remember the things you saw and in this remembrance there continues to be the quality of sight. The images in the mental life of a profoundly blind person are not visual. They lack perspective, colour, changes of shape as the object is turned around, decreasing size as the object is moved further away, and other similar features. Certainly, I have an image of my mobile phone but while it is three-dimensional, has a smooth metal casing and rows of buttons, I do not remember what I have seen when I think about it because I have never seen it. Instead, I remember what it feels like and sounds like. If you want to say that in feeling and remembering my mobile phone in this tactile way I am 'seeing' it, well and good, but remember that now you are using the word 'see' metaphorically.

I myself use the word 'see' in this way. When I say 'see you tomorrow' I do not expect to regain my sight but I do expect to be in your presence tomorrow. Why should I be deprived of the many uses of this metaphor simply because I can no longer use it literally? If someone in a wheelchair tells us that he or she intends to stand or run for election, we do not deny him or her the use of the metaphor, do we? We do not laugh and say, 'You mean you're going to sit for election.' The problem is that so much of our language is derived from the nature and use of our bodies. When your body is impaired, you become sharply aware of this, but it does not mean that you must stop using it. Many able-bodied people fear impairment, and thus many descriptions of impairment have acquired negative meanings and are used metaphorically to describe all sorts of unpleasant things. In the presence of disabled people, many able-bodied people become sensitive to the fact that the person with whom they are speaking can no longer use the language literally.

This is not the whole story of the Bible by any means. I appreciate the way that Yong discusses biblical people such as Jacob and

Job, showing how their disabled conditions were for the glory of God and for the ultimate enrichment of their own lives. In the writings of Paul there are many metaphors that recognise partial sight or even blindness as ways of describing the Christian life. We might think of seeing through a glass darkly[13] or of walking by faith not sight.[14] There is also Paul's beautiful theology of weakness, in which the strength of God is realised and the grace of God becomes all sufficient.[15]

There is no denying the fact, however, that the negative imagery of blindness and deafness has entered into our hymn books, often simply because of references to the Bible but reinforced by our everyday negative language. One hymn that used to be sung quite a lot is a veritable litany of disabilities.

> Lord, I was blind; I could not see
> In Thy marred visage any grace,
> But now the beauty of Thy face
> In radiant vision dawns on me.
>
> Lord, I was deaf; I could not hear
> The thrilling music of Thy voice;

[13] I Corinthians 13:12.

[14] 2 Corinthians 5:7.

[15] 2 Corinthians 12:9–10.

But now I hear Thee and rejoice,
And all Thine uttered words are dear!
Lord, I was dumb; I could not speak
The grace and glory of Thy name;
But now, as touched with living flame,
My lips Thine eager praises wake.

A more popular example is the hymn 'Amazing Grace':

Amazing Grace, how sweet the sound,
That saved a wretch like me.
I once was lost but now am found,
Was blind, but now I see.

Let us suppose that we changed the words as follows:

Amazing Grace, how sweet the sound,
That brought me to the light.
I once was lost but now am found,
Was black, but now I'm white.

Would this not be an outrageous example of racial prejudice? Would we not be ashamed to be asked to sing it? Then why do we not see that the line 'was blind but now I see' is equally negative towards blind people in equating their condition with unbelief, ignorance and sin? It is because society has been sensitised towards racism but the largely unconscious prejudice against disabled people is still unchallenged.

What can we do about all this? The problem is no different in the case of gender bias language. The modern hymn books are pretty good in replacing the use of 'man' and 'he' with more inclusive language. The same approach may be taken with the negative metaphors of disability. Where possible we improve the text; where this cannot be done, we do not sing that verse or even that hymn.

Blindness is not the only human condition which is treated in a negative manner in a number of biblical texts. Hannah Lewis, writing as a profoundly deaf person, speaks of the need to read the Bible as a deaf person, and proposes to create a 'Deaf Liberation hermeneutic'.[16] Just as in feminist theology women are claiming the Bible as their own and refusing to accept the exclusive male language, so groups of disabled people are protesting against the scriptures in so far as they are negative towards their lives. This has the effect of relativising the Bible. Feminists point out that it was written by men; blind people claim that on the whole the Bible expresses the points of view, including

[16] Hannah Lewis, *Deaf Liberation Theology*, Aldershot: Ashgate, 2007, pp. 105–31.

the prejudices, of the sighted community, and deaf people point out that it comes from the hearing world. In addition to the negative use of the metaphor of deafness, the Bible used in most of our churches is in the English language and can only be read as a text by those who know the English language and have learned to identify its alphabet. The Bible for people whose first language is British Sign Language would be a visual Bible, seen in video in bodily signs rather than being seen on a printed page.

How do these points of view affect popular Christian views about the authority and inspiration of the Bible? Thoughtful Christians today recognise that language, both spoken and written, always springs from a certain context. It is necessary to know something of that context in order to understand the meaning of the text. The books of the Bible also spring from a context. Indeed, the various documents which make up the Bible represent many different contexts. As its diversity is recognised, its status changes from an absolute infallible divine book into being the main conversational partner which engages the diverse worlds of Christian faith today. No other book can take the place of the Bible, but it will continue to challenge, inspire and instruct Christians today in so far as it is content to become our conversational partner and not our dictatorial master. This is a distinctively modern way of approaching the Bible but it is the only way in which the Bible in our culture can retain its energy as a living voice.

This chapter has been mainly negative. That is because we have been illustrating disability theology as a genre which seeks to expose the disadvantages which disabled people have suffered and protest against them. In addition to these biblical questions, there are much wider issues about the social and economic deprivations suffered by disabled groups. Disability theology becomes a natural partner of the disabled rights movement in its search for justice.

CHAPTER 3

Disability theology and the branches of theology: critical annunciation

We've seen that disability theology must denounce before it can announce, and in the previous chapter we discussed some examples of denunciation. It is time to move on to more positive aspects of disability theology, to announce good news to the church but also to carry out a critical evaluation of Christian doctrine. In so doing we shall leave the concept of genres behind us and consider the various branches of the Christian faith, asking how they may interact positively and negatively with the lives of both able and disabled people in the churches.

The obvious place to start is with Christian belief in God. When I started to read the Bible as a blind person I discovered that God is usually described as the God of light. God 'lives in unapproachable light, whom no one has seen or can see'.[17] At first I tried in vain to re-enter the realm of light in my imagination, but the more I tried the more distant God seemed. I received a handwritten letter from an elderly woman who said, 'For many years I have been gradually losing my sight. As I move from light into darkness, I feel that I am becoming increasingly remote from God.' I had discovered that there was a God of sighted people, who would take me back again if as a result of a miracle my sight was restored, to be in fellowship again with the one 'who has qualified you to share in the inheritance of his holy people in the kingdom of light. For he has rescued us from the dominion of darkness and brought us into the kingdom of the Son he loves.'[18]

Since it was impossible for me to re-enter the kingdom of light, I turned my attention to 'the dominion of darkness'. I wondered if there was a God of blind people, a God who would take me just as I am. I found a number of beautiful passages in the Bible where God is described as a God of darkness. I realised that God had said, 'I will give you hidden treasures, riches stored in secret places, so that you may

[17] I Timothy 6:16.

[18] Colossians I:12–13.

know that I am the LORD',[19] and I remembered that in the King James Version, God says, 'I will give thee the treasures of darkness.' I began to thank God for this strange and beautiful gift. Solomon said that 'The LORD has said that he would dwell in a dark cloud',[20] and again I called to mind the much more powerful expression of the King James Version that 'The LORD hath said that he would dwell in the thick darkness'. The reference to 'the thick darkness' made me wonder if the darkness was already there, and God had made it God's home. God was at home in the dark and so was I.

I found, however, that I could not entirely escape the negative power of the archetype of darkness, the ancient primal human memory of darkness as the unconscious, the abyss of nothingness. Then I discovered that beyond the world of light and the world of darkness there was a third realm which was beyond both these lower worlds. After all, if there is no light there is no darkness! I was beginning to move into a strange kind of human living where I was beyond light and darkness, and I discovered that this also was the place where God dwelt. 'If I say, "Surely the darkness will hide me and

[19] Isaiah 45:3.

[20] 2 Chronicles 6:1.

the light become night around me," even the darkness will not be dark to you; the night will shine like the day, for darkness is as light to you',[21] or, as the King James Version of my childhood memories described it, 'the darkness and the light are both alike to thee'. I realised that this was something a sighted person could never say, but for me and for God it was true. This meant that there was, after all, a God of totally blind people, and that my own life was stamped with the image of God not in spite of being blind but because of it.

For many people who believe in God, the onset of a disabling condition such as a severe stroke or Parkinson's disease not only brings about a challenging question about the purposes of God but it becomes a challenge to one's image of God. In fact, I believe that for most disabled people disability is a challenge to the imagination of faith rather than to the doctrines of the creed as such. Hannah Lewis and Wayne Morris[22] say that deaf people do not necessarily think of God as deaf but it is widely held in Christian deaf communities that God understands sign language. God is thought to communicate with deaf people

[21] Psalm 139:11–12.

[22] Wayne Morris, *Theology without Words: Theology in the deaf community*, Aldershot: Ashgate, 2006.

not through speech but through gestures and movements. Nevertheless, it remains true that on the whole the Bible describes God as a very fit, strong, able man. God has all the capacities of the human body but raised to a superhuman degree. So 'the eyes of the LORD range throughout the earth to strengthen those whose hearts are fully committed to him',[23] and 'The voice of the LORD is powerful; the voice of the LORD is majestic. The voice of the LORD breaks the cedars',[24] and, 'Your arm is endowed with power; your hand is strong, your right hand exalted.'[25]

Of course, we know that all these expressions are metaphors based upon the human body. They are an attempt to describe the greatness of God compared to humans. Nevertheless, as I said in Chapter 2, they are images taken from the able-bodied world and while not exactly denigrating the disabled body they might seem to place disabled people further from the image of God. The concept of human beings made in the image of God comes from Genesis 1:27. It has often been thought that the image of God is to be found in human reason, but this is not

[23] 2 Chronicles 16:9.

[24] Psalm 29:4–5.

[25] Psalm 89:13.

acceptable to a disability theology since people with severe intellectual disability would be excluded from being in the divine image. It is also often argued that since God is perfect, only those with perfect bodies can really be in God's image. In a way, this is even worse for a disability theology since it would leave so many people out. Most of us will lose a good deal of our former strength and beauty as we age and very few people do not have some minor ailment – so how perfect is perfect?

Perhaps we should think again about the image of God and try to imagine it in a much broader way. Yes, God is perfect but that does not mean that God is not capable of even more perfection. The concepts of the beauty of God and of God's love do not seem to entail any particular maximum. Love can grow more and more as more people are on the planet earth to be loved. Why should not God become more and more beautiful? It is true that nothing can surpass God but perhaps this does not apply to God! Only God can surpass God.

Perhaps when we think of God as being all-powerful we should remember that in Christian faith this means that God is fully capable of performing everything necessary to fulfil God's purposes. One of these is to create a world in which there are other beings with freedom – though infinitely less able and free than God. But the mere existence of genuine freedom outside God must surely mean that God withdraws some of God's own power in order, so to speak, to make room for the freedom of others. If the cosmos is not absolutely determined in advance but has a potential for novelty and chaos, then the Almighty One must have made it possible for novelty to exist alongside God's own endless novelty. Every human being experiences limitation. Everyone's body is limited: limited within a certain span of years, limited in having to live and work with other people who also have their desires and plans. Maybe God is also limited? Is God in some sense limited by the presence of an evil which, although not created by God, was at least allowed to be? If not, what are we to make of the many scriptural places which talk about God as a warrior, a hero involved in a struggle against evil powers?

I am suggesting that an uncritical idea of perfection can be a problem in Christian faith. We tend to think that God created everything perfect but things are now in a bit of a mess. Finally, however, everything will be perfect again. We need to recognise that there are many forms of perfection. Perfection itself may be diverse. So we should not try to divide people into those who are perfect and those who have an impairment, because basically we are all the same.

Creation

These thoughts about God lead us on to consider the creation. As we have seen, an overemphasis upon a sterile kind of perfection might lead us to consider human impairments as imperfections, and then to wonder about the wisdom of God in creation. The idea of perfection, however, must be associated with the idea of diversity, for God's creation is perfect exactly in the extraordinary diversity of life. It is when we build up a view of narrow normality that we begin to wonder about diversity. This conception of normality is reinforced by the advertising industry, the celebrity culture and the world of fashion to create an image of the normal person who is, in fact, far from being normal. The pressure to be normal can become quite oppressive, and many of us shrink from making friends with those who seem to us to be abnormal.

The liberating hope of the Kingdom of God calls us to be sceptical of 'normality' rather than being tempted to reject people who are different from us. Due to the loss of their habitats, the earth is losing many of its creatures and this process of extermination seems to be leading towards an unnatural standardisation of life, which parallels the cultural tendency towards conformity. While the market exhibits an amazing array of products, we are all under pressure to become standardised as consumers. As it accepts, welcomes and learns to love people of every kind and shape and language and orientation, the church becomes a prophetic witness against a narrow, disabling society.

God limited: Jesus Christ and human disability

In his sufferings and death, Jesus has been described as 'the disabled God'.[26] This powerful image has helped many disabled people to feel a closeness to Jesus which the older idea of Jesus as being a perfect young man with miraculous powers did little to help. Some people can't walk at all but Jesus walked on the water. Many of us can't put a couple of sentences together but Jesus spoke words of incomparable beauty and wisdom. Certainly, the reminder that even after his resurrection he was wounded and scarred is a striking thought, and does something to alleviate the almost inhuman perfection of Jesus.

[26] Nancy L. Eiesland, *The Disabled God: Toward a liberatory theology of disability*, Nashville, TN: Abingdon, 1994.

> A man there lived in Galilee
> like no one else before,
> for he alone from first to last
> our flesh unsullied wore;
> a perfect life of perfect deeds
> once to the world was shown,
> that everyone might mark his steps
> and in them place their own.[27]

But what is flesh unsullied? Another version of the hymn uses the word 'unblemished' but even in his resurrection and ascensions he was not unblemished. And was his flesh only something that he 'wore'? If this is the case, it is no wonder that 'death sought in vain to kill' him, as the third verse goes on to say, or, as it continues, how can we hope to place our footsteps in those of 'that brand, heroic, peerless soul'?

In the summer of 2008 I had a memorable conversation in a small Turkish village. My Muslim friend wanted to discuss the relative strengths and weaknesses of our two faiths. As he spoke of the grandeur, beauty and mercy of God I was full of admiration. After a while I asked him if he would like to sum up. He replied, 'My God does not snore. He does not

[27] Somerset Corry Lowry, 'A man there lived in Galilee'.

sweat, or walk the dusty streets.' I could only reply, 'But my God does.' According to Christian faith the saving reality of God in Christ was not his immediate and brilliant perfection but his emptying. Born out of wedlock into a peasant family, almost certainly an itinerant labourer, in him God accepted finitude, the limits of our humanity, our sufferings and our death. It is for this reason that we do not have an advocate who cannot be touched by our human griefs and infirmities but one who became like us that he might become our brother.[28]

There has been a great deal of discussion of the significance for disabled people of the healing miracles of Jesus. We must not allow the way our culture has conditioned us into normality to mislead us. It would be easy for us to think that Jesus took the distorted, abnormal people and normalised them, making them like everyone else. We should, rather, understand that the welcome Jesus extended to marginalised people, whether because of their occupation, their social status or their impairments, was an experience of healing. He healed people by helping them to escape the ritual taboos which marked them out as impure, by restoring them to the communities

28 Based on Hebrews 2:10–11; 4:15; and 5:8–10.

from which they had been banished, by eating and drinking with them when no one else would even touch them, and by restoring them to life in all its fullness. In many cases this healing process was accompanied by a cure, but it is the healing that we should emphasise, because it was being healed that saved them.

Because of the normalising oppression of our commodity culture with all of its competition, its rivalries and its badges of success, we are inclined to interpret the lonely, sick and excluded people Jesus met as examples of the much discussed medical model of disability. The medical model emphasises the plight of the individual, regarding disability as a personal tragedy to be overcome, if possible, by normalisation. The history of education's attempts to normalise deaf children by forbidding them to communicate in signs is an outstanding case of this. This is not to deny the healing power of the modern electronic wheelchair, or the amazing technology which enables someone like me to read. When I speak of the medical model I am referring to a socially constructed image or belief and not to the excellent work of rehabilitation medicine. What I want to emphasise is that I value reading not because of the extraordinary technology which makes it possible but because it enables me to converse with the philosophers, theologians, poets and novelists of all ages. It includes me within the human community. I rather think that the same is true of people using modern wheelchairs. One is grateful for the wheelchair because of what it does rather than just because of what it is. This is nothing but common sense. The wheelchair sports in the Paralympics bear witness to this. Without the equipment it would not be possible, and this is true of cricket and football, whoever plays them. But what is valued is the joy of the sport, the inclusion within the sporting community.

Too much of the discussion about the healing work of Jesus has focused upon them as miracles. No doubt this was an important feature in the days long ago when miracles were looked upon as supernatural proof of the divinity of Jesus Christ. Today, when we have come to understand a little more (but still not much) about the healing powers of the charismatic shaman in many primal cultures, we can see that the good news for our culture is not, as children are inclined to say, that Jesus did magic tricks but that he created a community of inclusive love.

We have been discussing the implications for disability theology of various doctrinal branches of Christian faith, such as belief in God, creation and the person and work of Jesus Christ. There is much more which could be said but we must now go on to discuss the third of the theological types into which we can place disability theology. We can now consider it as a frontier theology.

CHAPTER 4

Disability theology as a frontier theology: people with disabilities and the prophetic church

The job of a frontier theology is to engage Christian faith with something which is not in itself Christian. It is important to stress that the frontier of engagement is not with a reality that is not religious, but only with that which is not overtly Christian; after all, Christian faith itself affirms that the Spirit of God is at work everywhere and that God is in all things. The task of frontier theology is to express the innate or implicit religious quality of all things in terms of explicit Christian faith. When we seek to construct a theology of world religions, we do not deny that the unknown Christ may be in every faith, but as soon as we give the name 'Jesus Christ' to this unknown, we are doing frontier theology.

There will be two main aspects of our discussion. We will first consider Christian faith as good news for disabled people and then we will consider disabled people as being good news to the church and for society.

The prosperity gospel and the miraculous cure

There are forms of Christian faith that have become completely captivated by the medical model of disability. Christians of this kind are strengthened in their faith when they see, or think they see, evidence of miraculous healing or a type which in scientific and medical terms is inexplicable. It is the ineffable quality of the miraculous, the very fact that it is inexplicable, which arouses their faith. Such Christians tend to draw a sharp line between the natural and the supernatural. For them, God dwells in the supernatural and enters into the secular to transform it by means which are beyond the understanding of the secular.

I do not deny that there may be cultures in which this world view is held with such strong social coherence that miracles of this kind may sometimes work. It may also be true that this was the world view of first-century Palestine, and continues to be prevalent in parts of Africa and Asia, for example. But it was not the world view of modernity and it is not the dominant world view in our own postmodern cultures. That is not to deny that there may be enclaves of this supernaturalistic or occult faith in our modern western world. After all, Christian faith itself of whatever kind has to some extent become an enclave, a cognitive minority.

I am sure of this, that where these occult enclaves survive in Christian congregations they cause great suffering and distress to many disabled people. I have known Christians who, having lost their sight, felt that they had been hounded from one congregation to another by the expectation that as Christians they would receive their sight back. I myself would feel uncomfortable if I went to a healing service in a church because I cannot resist feeling that some, perhaps many, people would imagine or wonder whether I had come in the hope of getting my sight back. I find this possibility sufficiently embarrassing and intrusive to keep me away from healing services. It is because of this kind of insensitive injection of a first-century cosmology into the life of the modern congregation that many disabled people, like many gay people, have felt unwelcome in the church, and it is because of this that secular disability rights advocates will sometimes say that Christian faith, the church and the Bible do not offer answers to disabled people but only create more problems.

I call it the medical model in theological dress because disabled people are treated as tragically afflicted individuals. The model assumes it is they, the disabled ones, who have to change and does not realise that it is the society which has to change. It does not realise that such churches have become reflections of the world of capitalist economies, where individual success is the prize of life and to compete in the marketplace one must be normal, where normal means rich. The gospel of the miraculous cure is the prosperity gospel for disabled people. How alluring it is! That quiet voice whispers, 'Why not try it? You have nothing to lose but your pride.' But there is a more excellent way, a way of faith, hope and love.

The gospel for people with disabilities

The gospel for people with disabilities is that there is no gospel with particular reference to their disability as such. The good news is that they are accepted by God and by the church in their disability, and not in spite of it but in all of its human diversity. The same is true of gay people. Some say that the gospel for gay people is that they should become straight.

The same is sometimes said of people with disabilities. The gospel is preached to them as if it was disability which was their problem and the gospel would take their disability away by a miracle. The way gay people have often heard Christian faith has been distorted by the negativity with which the church has regarded them. What has created the difficulty is not their sexual orientation or even the gospel, but the attitudes in the church which they have all too often encountered. In the same way, there is no special gospel addressed to disabilities, apart from the gospel of welcome. The whole point of the inclusive church is that gay people are accepted as gay people and people with disabilities are accepted as people.

The same is true in some ways of feminist theology. It was a man's Bible and a man's church and women were made to feel that they had to put feminine characteristics behind them and act like a man, although even that was scarcely permitted. The gospel for women is therefore that their femininity as such is not a problem. They are accepted on an equal footing with men; indeed, it is the richness of both the feminine and the masculine which contributes to the rich diversity of the body of Christ.

When we were talking about theology of

film as a frontier theology, we saw that film itself was not the problem; it was a matter of interpreting it, or bringing it so to speak within and under the lordship of Christ. In a somewhat similar way we have seen that when we consider disability theology as a kind of frontier theology, we discover that disability itself is not a problem. What faith does is to grasp people with disabilities and pull them into the body of Christ, where, as Paul says, the parts that were sometimes looked down on are now given the highest honours.[29] That is not to say that living as a disabled person does not present all kinds of problems and challenges but it is to claim that disability itself is not a theological problem. I have tried to show that it is the language and the attitudes of society, and even of the Bible and the church, which have construed disabled conditions as being theological problems. I have tried to show that people with disabilities are part of the rich variety of God's creation, that God may be found within the disabled conditions, and that the gospel of inclusion receives them on an equal footing. The closing words of the New Testament remain true for all human beings: 'Whosoever will, may come.'[30]

[29] I Corinthians 12:22–23

[30] Revelation 22:17

The prophetic calling of disabled people in the church

The gospel for people with disabilities is more than welcome, more than inclusion. Disabled people have a distinct ministry in the church. Disabled people are not so much a pastoral problem as a prophetic potential. We need to ask not how the church can care for disabled people but to ask what is the prophetic message of the church in our culture and how disabled people can make a unique contribution to that renewal. This is not to value disabled people because of what we are supposed to be able to learn from them, such as their alleged courage, patience and cheerfulness. That would be to make instrumental use of disabled people. My question is not what we have to learn from disabled people but how the whole church can respond to its evangelical calling and how disabled people can not only participate in this but can become witnesses to and leaders of it.

This involves a change in the church's understanding of itself and its mission. As long as the emphasis within the church is for its own growth, prosperity and increased popularity, it becomes a mirror of normal society. As long as the Christian gospel deals mainly with the individual happiness of believers, it will fail to find its prophetic voice. So much of the life and worship of the church has become little more than a celebration of its own belief structure and a habitual repetition of my salvation, my Jesus, our God. This emphasis upon ownership and interior possession again models Christian faith upon the consuming culture where faith itself has become a satisfying product to be consumed again and again because of the happiness and comfort which it brings. Is there then no peace and joy in believing? There certainly is, but it is a by-product of the prophetic mission not its goal.

In a world ruled by the money god, the church of Jesus Christ must become counter-cultural. The Bible, which continues to be the wellspring of the life of the church, is itself profoundly countercultural. Of course, one might suggest that the trouble with the Bible is that it points both ways in the struggle between the rich and the poor, and one might wonder what we are to make of a Bible which contains documents written by and about kings. But the remarkable thing about the Bible is that however great the pressure from the surrounding imperial culture, the voice of the marginalised and the poor is never completely silenced. It is for this reason, among others, that the Bible is rightly regarded as the Word of God. Indeed, the great American prophetic biblical commentator Daniel Berrigan has shown that even the books entitled 'Kings' are the products of the prophetic tradition, seeking not to glorify them but to show what a disaster the monarchy was for the covenant between Israel and God.[31]

The Bible is the story of how God chose a group of slaves, and formed them into a nation, not a great nation or a powerful one but a small nation pressed throughout its entire history between the greater imperial powers. The Bible shows a God who is partial to the oppressed and to the excluded, describing a God who loves justice and who uses the nothings of this world to confound the mighty. People with disabilities have a particular role in enabling the church to be itself, not exactly because of their disabilities, but because of the way that their impairments have been turned into disabilities by a society which has been given over to the beautiful, the rich and the powerful, and by a church which instead of living biblical values has allowed itself to become normalised. In other words, in order for the church to be the church, people with disabilities should accept the church and try to change it from within. There is not so much a question of including

[31] Daniel Berrigan, *The Kings and their Gods: The pathology of power*, Grand Rapids: Eerdmans, 2008.

disabled people in the church; it is rather a matter of the normal church learning how to welcome those who appear to be different, and in that welcome which embraces difference to rediscover the prophetic calling.[32] The church will become more truly a symbol of the Kingdom of God when it becomes more faithfully a community of inclusive love.

[32] John M. Hull, *Towards the Prophetic Church*, London: SCM Press, 2014.

PART 3

Resources

WENDY BRYANT

This resource section will help your church consider how some of the issues raised in the book can be taken further. Here you will find practical suggestions, as well as details about key organisations and suggested further reading.

This section has been written by Wendy Bryant. After working for several years as a social worker with people with learning disabilities, Wendy lived and worked with Kaleidoscope Theatre, in community with young adults with Down's syndrome. Wendy has worked as Disability Adviser for the Dioceses of Guildford and Oxford, and is currently Open to All (Disability) Adviser for the Diocese of Bath and Wells.

For further reflection with your church

John M. Hull has argued eloquently that disabled people have a distinct ministry in the church, and that the church is only whole when all are included.

We all want our churches to be places of welcome for everyone, and generally believe that they are. However, there may well be unintended barriers, visible or invisible, which exclude some people, and in particular people with disabilities. In seeking to remove or reduce these barriers, we need to understand the breadth of the term 'disability', which includes sensory or mobility impairment, learning disability, mental health problems, autism, and hidden disabilities, for example epilepsy, arthritis, dyslexia, dyspraxia, diabetes, and many others. And of course many people have more than one impairment, and live with the effects of the interplay of a number of conditions.

All churches have a duty under the Equality Act 2010 to review their accessibility for people with disabilities and to do all things reasonable to remove any barriers. Key points to remember in this process are:

- to involve disabled people at every stage;
- to understand that disabled people may be ministers or leaders, as well as members;
- that 'people with disabilities' are all different, all individual, and that even people with the same impairment will have different experiences of living with it;
- that there is much that can be done at little or no cost. For example, ensuring that your notice sheets, church magazines etc. comply with clear print guidelines, and that all steps and changes of level are clearly marked with contrasting colour, will greatly assist people with visual impairment;
- that an individual's access to a building should be independent, where this is appropriate to their age. We like to be helpful and 'help' a wheelchair user down the steps into church, but this should be avoided if at all possible; apart from being a safety risk to all involved, it can diminish the independence and dignity of the person.

Organisations you may find helpful

There are several Christian organisations which offer information and resources on disability inclusion for churches. Most of these organisations have local branches with their own activities.

- **Contact a Family**
  www.cafamily.org.uk
  An excellent source of information, advice and resources on family life with a disabled child. Not a church-based organisation, but an invaluable resource.

- **Go! Sign**
  www.gosign.org.uk
  Aims to support deaf Christians in their church experience and to bring the gospel to deaf people.

- **L'Arche**
  www.larche.org.uk
  An international movement which builds faith-based communities all over the world: places of welcome where people are transformed by the experience of community, relationship, disability and difference.

- **Livability**
  www.livability.org.uk
  The UK's largest disability charity, offering information, resources and accommodation enabling disabled people to live independent lives.

- **Open Ears**
  www.openears.org.uk
  A Christian charity which supports people with hearing impairment.

- **Prospects**
  www.prospects.org.uk
  A Christian organisation working together with people with learning disabilities so they live life to the full. It offers many useful resources.

- **The Kairos Forum**
  www.thekairosforum.com
  Seeks to highlight and respond to the spiritual and religious needs of people with intellectual and cognitive disabilities.

- **Through the Roof**
  www.throughtheroof.org
  Works with people with disabilities in the UK and abroad to 'transform lives through disabled people'. It has many useful resources.

- **Torch Trust**
  www.torchtrust.org
  Provides Christian resources and activities for blind and visually impaired people in the UK and worldwide.

Resources to help make church buildings accessible

- **Centre for Accessible Environments**
  www.cae.org.uk
  The UK's leading authority on inclusive design of the built environment.

- **The Church Buildings Council**
  www.churchcare.co.uk
  The Church of England's resource to support the care of buildings.

- John Penton, *Widening the Eye of the Needle: Access to church buildings for people with disabilities*, 3rd edn, London: Church House Publishing, 2008.

Further reading

Archbishops' Council, *Opening the Doors: Ministry with people with learning disabilities and people on the autistic spectrum*, London: General Synod of the Church of England, 2009. A clear and practical guide for churches to enable people with learning disabilities to be more fully included in the life and worship of the church.

Simon Bass, *Special Children Special Needs: Integrating children with disabilities and special needs into your church*, London: Church House Publishing, 2003. Good practice guidelines and practical ideas for teaching and nurture for children with disabilities in church life.

Brian Brock and John Swinton, *Disability in the Christian Tradition: A reader*, Grand Rapids, MI: Eerdmans, 2012. A collection of theological reflections on disability and its meaning in society and in the church down the ages.

Donald Eadie, *Grain in Winter*, London: Epworth, 1999, reprinted 2007. A collection of reflections, prayers and meditations from a diverse range of people living with pain or impairment; those who travel with them, and others who take on the pain of the world in some way.

John Gillibrand, *Disabled Church – Disabled Society: The implications of autism for philosophy, theology and politics*, London: Jessica Kingsley, 2010. Writing from personal experience of caring for his autistic son, and drawing on his study of philosophy, the author presents challenging reflections on faith and the care of the most vulnerable in our society.

John M. Hull, *In the Beginning there was Darkness: A blind person's conversation with the Bible*, London: SCM Press, 2001. A fascinating and stimulating discussion of response to the Bible from the perspective of blindness.

John M. Hull, *The Tactile Heart: Blindness and faith*, London: SCM Press, 2013. A collection of theological essays which relate blindness and faith, and develop a theology of blindness which makes a constructive contribution to the field of disability theology.

Roy McCloughry, *The Enabled Life: Christianity in a disabling world. Including a conversation with Jean Vanier*, London: SPCK, 2013. Writing from personal experience of living with a hidden disability, the author puts the case for disabled people being at the heart of the church and God's Kingdom.

Roy McCloughry and Wayne Morris, *Making a World of Difference: Christian reflections on disability*, London: SPCK, 2002. A good basic introduction to the relationship between disability and the Christian faith.

Tony Phelps-Jones et al., *Making Church Accessible to All: Including disabled people in church life*, Abingdon: Bible Reading Fellowship, 2013. Clear guidance on practical ways of making teaching, worship and buildings accessible for people with a variety of impairments.

John Swinton and Elaine Powrie, *Why Are We Here? Meeting the spiritual needs of people with learning disabilities*, London: Mental Health Foundation, 2004 . Study based on interviews with people with learning disabilities. Contains good accessible-language summaries, and challenges for the church in including people with learning disabilities.

Gordon Temple with Lin Ball, *Enabling Church: A Bible-based resource towards the full inclusion of disabled people*, London: SPCK, 2012. A practical resource for church groups who wish to explore issues of disability inclusion in our churches.

Martin Lloyd Williams, *Beauty and Brokenness: Compassion and the Kingdom of God*, London: SPCK, 2007. An exploration of the relationship between creation and humanity, inspired by the author's family experience of disability.

Amos Yong, *The Bible, Disability and the Church*, Grand Rapids, MI: Eerdmans, 2011. A comprehensive biblical theology of disability which challenges some traditional interpretations.

Index